The Art of
Embroidered
Flowers

D0995699

To the memory of Gilda's dear mother,
Eve Rothaul. She was an inspiration to
all who met her.

The Art of
Embroidered
Flowers

Gilda Baron

SEARCH PRESS

First published in Great Britain 2004

This edition published in 2017

Search Press Limited
Wellwood, North Farm Road,
Tunbridge Wells, Kent TN2 3DR

ISBN 978-1-78221-522-6

The Publishers and author can accept no responsibility for
any consequences arising from the information, advice or
instructions given in this publication.

If you have difficulty in obtaining any of the materials and
equipment mentioned in this book, please visit the Search
Press website for details of suppliers:
www.searchpress.com

Alternatively, you can write to the publishers at the
address above for a current list of stockists, including
firms which operate a mail-order service.

Publisher's note
All the step-by-step photographs in this book
feature the author, Gilda Baron, demonstrating
how to create embroidered gardens and
landscapes. No models have been used.

Colour separation by Classiscan Pte Ltd., Singapore
Printed in Malaysia by Times Offset (M) Sdn Bhd

*I would like to thank Caroline Munns of
Rainbow Silks, for supplying the fabric dyes
and paints for this book; and Coats Anchor
Threads, for their generosity in supplying
many of the threads.*

Front cover

Glow Over the Lake
Size: 45 x 30cm (17½ x 12in)
*All the methods used to produce
this piece are shown in this book.*

Page 1

Poppy Basket
size: 18 x 20cm (7 x 8in)
*This picture was machine stitched
on to hand-made paper.*

Pages 2–3

Sunset Over the Foothills
size: 44 x 29cm (17¼ x 11½in)
*For panoramic scenes like this, see
pages 76–77.*

Page 5

Lavender and Lace
Detail – see also page 70
*Using lace instead of circles cut
from cotton to make the flowers
can produce interesting effects.*

Contents

Introduction

I have always gained pleasure from being creative. I began to draw and sew at a very early age, and I have not lost any of the excitement and pleasure it gives me. Friends ask why I do not spend more time doing nothing, but I would be unbearable to live with if I did! I relax with fabric, threads and dyes, or a pencil and pad.

I started my career as a designer and pattern cutter in the fashion industry, but when my children were young I switched to teaching, mainly in adult education. It taught me a great deal about how to bring many simple skills together and help students to develop unique pieces of work, whether it was a dress, hat or cushion or embroidery.

Since I decided to give up lecturing full time and devote more time to my own creativity, I have not looked back. All my skills came together: hand and machine sewing; embroidery; fabric dyeing; batik; drawing and painting, and it is a joy to be able to do these wonderful things. I do have moments of frustration: we all have off-days, and sewing machines and other tools can go wrong. But we learn from our mistakes and it is especially rewarding to overcome problems and produce a good, creative piece of work. Some of my most interesting pieces of work have emerged from the process of finding ways of rescuing them.

This book is just a springboard for your own creative development, so let it take you down your own paths. Do not expect your work to look exactly the same as mine. I never produce two identical pieces: dyes perform differently, colours may be a shade lighter or darker. The techniques shown are starting points, not blueprints.

I have included a project with machine embroidery, but if you do not have, or do not want to use, a sewing machine just hand-stitch it instead. If you use techniques you are not happy with, it will show in your work. Do not worry; let it happen. It may be only a piece of fabric or paper, but you will be surprised how it will seem to shout at you to stitch on it. That is the creative fun of it, and I hope you get as much joy from creating your works of art as I do. Have fun!

Gilda

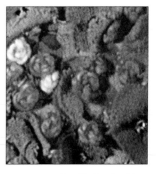

Detail of embroidery

Materials & equipment

You will need only the minimum of equipment to begin. Many of the things you need can be found around the average house, and I use only the basic materials: dyes, fabric pens, cotton fabric, and threads. In time, you may want to be more adventurous and add to your stock of materials. All the methods used in this book can be carried out on a kitchen table or work surface.

Fabric and paper

Fine pure cotton poplin or medium weight cotton lawn absorb the dyes well. Manufacturers sometimes coat fabric with dressing so it looks crisper and more attractive. If left in, this dressing will absorb the dyes, and they will wash out the first time the fabric is washed. If in doubt wash your material first. Iron out any creases before starting to dye. Some fabric that looks like cotton has polyester added to stop it creasing. If it contains more than 10% polyester, the dyes will not take as well, so check carefully: the higher the percentage of man-made fibre, the paler the dye. On 100% man-made fabric the dye may not take at all. Always test the fabric to make sure it will absorb the dyes. They may run faster on some fabric if it is very absorbent. You may have to spray less-absorbent fabric lightly with water until it is damp, to encourage the dyes to flow.

Wadding is used behind designs to give the work some body. It may also need backing fabric but this need not be pure cotton. Absorbent paper can be placed under the fabric before you dye it to make 'bonus' backgrounds – see page 62. Choose good quality paper that stays strong when wet, without texture if you do not want the fabric to pick up any pattern. All-purpose household cloths are used under fabric when

dyeing and painting to stop it sticking. Paint or dye will stain them, but they can be washed and used again. Hand-made paper can be used to mount designs – see page 74 for details.

The cotton lawn fabric, wadding, backing fabric, absorbent paper, all-purpose household cloth and hand-made paper used in the projects are all easily obtained.

Threads

I use ordinary sewing threads, as well as threads made specially for machine embroidery. Mix the different threads to give a variety of textures and colour to your work. Over the years I have accumulated large quantities of thread of all kinds, so I try to keep them stored by colour. It can sometimes be difficult to decide whether the pinkish mauve should be stored with the pink or the mauve, or whether the reddish brown goes with red or brown, but using clear polythene bags means I can usually spot what I need.

Hand-sewing threads

I try to store these by colour, too, using a box with compartments. This can be difficult, as I have so many that I have dyed myself, and I have to confess that my box is not always as organised as it should be. If you are unsure about the thread, try it out on a small area for colour and texture. Hand stitch can easily be taken out if you decide you do not like the results.

Machine threads

You can use any weight of machine thread for embroidery, so look first for the most suitable colours, then lay them on the dyed fabric and see which blend in the best. They may not always be the ones you thought of first. Some of the variegated threads may look just right on the reel, but when you unwind them a little they can look very different. I often use variegated machine threads that have a mixture of colour or shades in one reel. There are also some wonderful metallic and textured sewing machine threads. If you are machining a large area, make sure you have enough thread to complete the job, unless you are lucky enough to have a shop selling threads nearby.

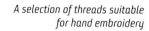

A selection of threads suitable for hand embroidery

Threads suitable for use on a sewing machine

Dyes and paints

In this book, I will just be using silk dyes and fabric paints. These are the easiesl to use, but still give good and interesting results. I will also show you ways to introduce other simple to use products to enhance your work.

Silk dyes These are very liquid, run and flow when applied, and can be used on most natural fabrics. Choosing iron-fix dyes will simplify the process: some need more complicated steam-fixing. You will need only a few colours: mix one or more to make the shade you want, or dilute with water to make paler shades. The dyes are translucent, so yo u can put one colour on top of another to make a third colour. Mix fresh dye for each project, and follow the manufacturer's instructions.

Fabric/textile paints These have a thicker consistency and can be used for painting, spongeing, stencilling and block printing. They can also be diluted with water and used like silk dyes, or you can spray the fabric lightly with water before applying them to make them run. Some types may make the fabric stiff if too many layers of paint are used. Many fabric paints need to be heat-fixed, and should be ironed from the back following the manufacturer's instructions. They are usually recommended only for use on cotton.

NOTE

If you want to work on dark fabrics, you will need special fabric paints. These are similar to regular fabric paints, but have pigments in them so that they sit on the surface of the fabric. They will not sink into the dark areas, or be absorbed and vanish into the dark background. Alternatively, you could mix white or silver fabric paint into regular fabric paints.

Other useful paints

Glittery, pearly, shiny and fluorescent paints can add interest to your work. Some fabric paints are available in tubes with a nozzle, and can be squeezed out in straight lines or to follow outlines. Follow the individual manufacturers' instructions for fixing.

I use an inexpensive palette from a children's store. I find the colour-coded individual pots useful when I am mixing my dyes.

Opposite
Purple Sky

My inspiration comes from my sketch book, which contains many memories of the colour of skies and of light. I used silk dyes to obtain the purples and blues of the sky, then added yellows and greens to the lower part. With fabric pens, I created some interesting areas to machine and hand stitch on top of.

Other equipment

Sewing machine You do not have to embroider any of the designs in this book by machine. If you choose to, you will not need an expensive or complicated model, though it is an advantage if your machine will work zig-zag stitch.

Brushes You do not have to buy expensive artists' brushes, but keep a range of sizes. Use a fan brush to produce interesting effects, to add small amounts of dye to create dramatic skies, or load it with fabric paint and drag it across your work.

Fabric pen These come in a range of sizes and thicknesses and usually look like felt tip pens. All are suitable for cotton, but some can be used for other fabrics too. Most need fixing with an iron.

Sponge Tear or cut these into small, irregular pieces and use them for printing. Natural sponge is the best but cheaper synthetic sponge is also suitable. Sponges can be rinsed and re-used even if they are stained.

Salt Sprinkle this on wet silk dyes to create interesting shapes and textures. Dishwasher salt is a good, far cheaper alternative to manufactured discharge salt.

Masking tape This has many uses, so keep wide and narrow reels at hand.

Hairdryer Use this to help to dry your work more quickly.

Iron Keep an electric iron handy at all times for pressing your work.

Pots or jars Use these for mixing dyes and rinsing brushes.

Scrap paper You will need this to protect your work surface. Newspaper is ideal.

Dressmaking pins Use these to attach the wadding or paper to your fabric.

Sewing needles You will need a variety of sizes to tack your work into place, and also to embroider birds on your pictures.

Embroidery needles The size will depend on the thread you use, but you will need some with very big eyes.

Scissors Use a small sharp pair to cut threads and another pair to cut paper.

Needle threader These are useful if your eyes are not as young as they were.

Palette Small china or plastic palettes are useful for mixing paints and dyes.

Dropper This is useful for transferring dye to your mixing palette.

Embroidery hoop I prefer the ones with metal springs, but those with screws are also fine.

Elastic bands Use these to fasten the ends of threads when dyeing them.

Bubble wrap This can be used to produce interesting print effects.

Tape measure You will need this to measure fabric and mounts etc.

Ring reinforcements and assorted stickers Use these to mask out small areas of your work.

NOTE
You can spray fabric protector (not shown) on completed work to protect it from grease and dirt. Some types also offer some protection from light rays (UVA).

13

Design

Designs can be planned in advance if you prefer, but be flexible and do not panic if the dye runs into other colours, or turns out a shade darker than you wanted. You might like to give yourself some visual guidelines, perhaps by making small pencil marks on the outer edges of your fabric. I would not advise using pencil marks in the area you plan to work on as they may show on the finished piece.

I am sometimes clumsy, and drip some colour where it should not be. If this happens, there is usually a way to disguise it. Just draw in a few more blades of grass with fabric pens, or add a few extra French knots on the appropriate place! This is where the words 'artistic licence' are most relevant, and nobody but yourself need know.

One useful tip is to work on a larger piece of fabric than you need, so that you can choose the best area afterwards, perhaps with the help of a mount.

Using photographs

When I am on holiday, or out and about I take photographs of places, the countryside and the coastline. These photographs of interesting scenes are useful aids to the memory and help me to remember the colours and shapes of flowers. This is all I need, as I only want an impression of flowers, not an accurate interpretation.

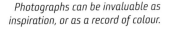

Photographs can be invaluable as inspiration, or as a record of colour.

Wild Irises

The photographs opposite helped to provide colour reference for this embroidery.

I always feel lucky that I live in the British Isles. Our changeable weather is always a talking point, but this is why we have such varied and amazing skies: sometimes grey; sometimes blue, often a breathtaking mixture of colours and cloud shapes.

I do sometimes sketch skies, but this can be difficult as the clouds can move fast, or the colours of the sunset can change before your eyes. This is when I think the camera needs to come out to capture that moment in time.

Inspirational photographs like these help me to paint beautiful skies.

Opposite

Red Sky at Night

Size: 25.5 x 33cm (10 x 13in)

The lovely red sky lasts only a short time, so I tried to capture it by dyeing the background with a deep red silk dye and adding small touches of black. When it was dry, I placed a piece of masking tape horizontally across the middle of the work, dabbing black fabric paint over the top edge. After drying the work and removing the masking tape, I added green fabric paint to the lower areas and hand and machine stitched on to this.

Using sketchbooks

Photographs are an invaluable source or reference material, but in some ways the quick sketches I make at the same time are even more important. When I look at these, I can remember what the weather was like, who I was with and even the location, in fact everything about the day's sights and smells, because the sketches are somehow part of me and what I create.

Many times over the years I have heard students cry: 'I am not artistic'. You do not need any artistic skill to produce a beautiful piece of embroidery, but you may be more talented than you think. It is only recently that I have found the courage to show my sketch book to people. I used to believe, wrongly, that as I had not been to art school, I could not draw.

Buy a sketch book and a few pencils. Take them out with you, and try to capture the sky, flowers, leaves or the landscape. I can already hear some of you screaming: 'But I can't draw'. Do not worry: you can still put down the colours you can see. You only need a few scribbled lines of colour to remind you of the sunset, or the reds, yellows and browns of autumn. It will help you to look and see, rather than just look. You will be surprised how much more you see when you start drawing. If you lack confidence, remember you are doing it just for yourself: you do not need to show your drawings to anyone.

Just try to follow a few tips, especially from nature. Look closely at flowers: if you magnify a petal, you will be surprised how many colours you find Sometimes these colours are completely unexpected: yellows, pinks and oranges may all be blended into what looks like a simple pink rose. When you feel a little braver, you might want try a few interesting shapes, or draw a single leaf or petal. Do not attempt anything too complicated, just keep it simple. In time, you may feel ready to go a little further and draw a whole plant, or capture a sunset and clouds. It really is not important how good they are, they will be your memories.

If you have no time to make a proper sketch, use the pencils to scribble the colours in your sketchbook for quick reference.

Shades of Purple

Size: 45 x 30cm (17½ x 12in)

If it is cold, wet or my time is limited, I use my sketch book to capture just the colours I see for quick reference. I used this method to capture these lovely mauves and purples.

Layers of dye, fabric pen and machine-stitched lines give depth to this moody picture. The background was dyed with shades of violet and purple, with black added for the hills and green in the foreground. The fabric for the flowers was dyed with a mixture of these colours. The background was machine embroidered with hand stitching and flowers added.

Techniques

Making a start is easy as long as you remember there are no rules! This is your own piece of work, and you can add as much colour as you like to it. The dyes will do things for you that they may not do for others.

Backgrounds

The background for your embroidery is painted first, then the stitches are added. This is a magical process: when you apply the dyes to fabric, things will just happen. They grow and spread, often producing unexpected but wonderful shapes and colours – a bit like nature. Reds and blues will run and blend to produce shades of mauve. Blues and yellows will run and give you shades of green. Your first piece should be treated as an experiment: you need to experience how the dyes flow and learn how thickly to apply the fabric paint. Then you can begin to judge how much dye you need to use to achieve what you want. The most important thing to remember is not to worry. Relax. Just let it happen.

You will need

· Pure cotton fabric
  36 x 46 cm (14 x 18in)
· Silk dye in turquoise and purple
· Black fabric pen
· Flat 13mm (½in) wash brush
· Masking tape
· Non-woven all-purpose
  household cloth
· Scrap paper or newspaper
· Iron
· Hairdryer
· Absorbent paper (optional)
· Old brush
· Pink fabric paint

The pink fabric paint and blue and purple silk dyes used for the project

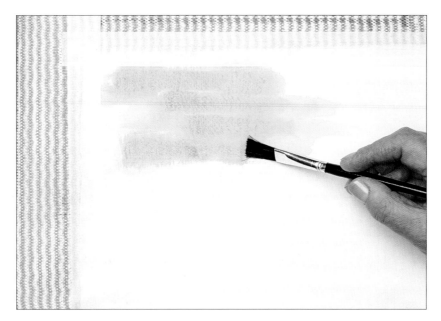

1 Press the fabric. Protect your work surface with scrap paper or newspaper and lay all-purpose household cloth on top. Lay the fabric on top and secure it with masking tape. Mix the dyes you want to use for the background by diluting with water, testing them on a spare piece of fabric and remembering that they will dry lighter. Using a 13mm (½in) wash brush and starting at the top, paint on the turquoise silk dye with long, sweeping strokes.

NOTE

If you place absorbent paper under the fabric before you start to work, you could end up with a 'bonus' background that you can use for cards and pictures – see page 62 for ideas. Remember that this is optional.

2 Continue until you have covered your fabric. Do not worry about going right to the edge because it will be covered by a mount when your work is finished.

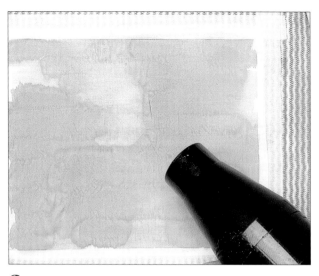

3 Let your work dry, or use a hairdryer to speed up the process. Hold it at least 30cm (12in) away from your work – if it is held too close it may overheat and cut out.

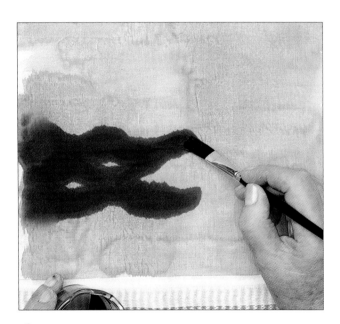

4 Using the wash brush, paint on the undiluted purple dye using wavy strokes as shown. Leave your work to dry for about an hour or so – it is difficult to give a precise time, as it will depend on the temperature and humidity.

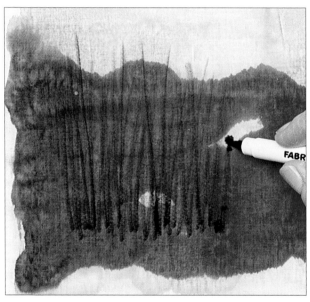

5 When your work is dry, use a black fabric pen to put in the stalks of the grasses with sweeping upward strokes.

Printed backgrounds

Shapes printed on a painted fabric background with ordinary bubble wrap can be used to suggest flowers.

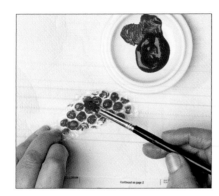

6 Use a brush to apply thick pink fabric paint to a small piece of cut bubble wrap.

7 Turn the bubble wrap over and use it to print circles on to the fabric. These will represent flowers. Continue until you are happy with the effect.

The finished background

Let your work dry, then press from the back to set the paint and dyes. It can be framed and mounted as it is – see page 25 – or embroidery can be added.

Adding embroidery

Lay a selection of threads on your work to help you choose the best colours.

NOTE

Try using different sizes of bubble wrap. Supermarket fruit and vegetable sections sometimes have interesting bubble wrap and are usually happy for you to take it.

When printing with bubble wrap, try using more than one shade of paint.

Further backgrounds

These backgrounds were painted with only one colour of silk dye, in this case turquoise. A pale wash of the colour was applied to the whole background using a 13mm (½in) wash brush. Then a deeper shade of the same colour was applied using a fan brush, which gives a softer edge.

Grasses were drawn in with black, green and purple fabric pens.

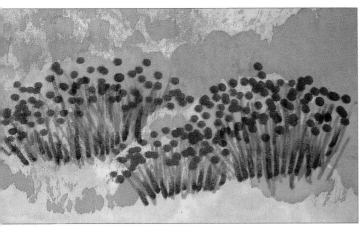

Grass stems were drawn with black and purple fabric pens, then the tip of the purple pen was used to draw dots to represent flowers.

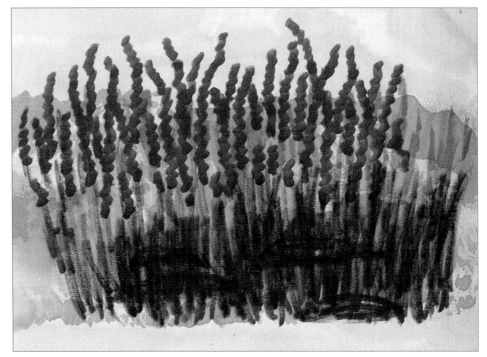

Black and green fabric pens were used for the grasses, with a purple fabric pen used above, but this time I drew the 'flowers' using a wavy line.

Presenting your work

Good presentation is just as important as the work itself. I first select the area of work I want to use, then I cut it out and stiffen it simply by tacking it to two or three layers of lightweight paper, making sure it lies flat.

Selecting an area

Choose a mount that complements the embroidery. Cream is usually safest, though even this can look wrong against a picture with a lot of white. Lay the mount over the work and select the area you want to use carefully. You may feel that you need more sky, or that the composition is improved by turning the mount horizontally. Move it round until you decide which area is best.

You will need

· Aperture mount
· Masking tape
· Lightweight paper
  (photocopier paper is ideal)
· Scissors
· Needle and tacking thread

1 Select the area you want to use for your finished picture...

2 ...trying out portrait and landscape format mounts for different effects.

Mounting

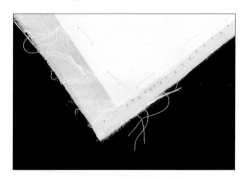

3 Tack your work to two or three layers of thin paper.

4 Trim off excess fabric and attach the work to the mount with masking tape.

NOTE

Small left-over pieces of work can be used to make greetings cards (see page 62).

Framing

A good way to display your work is to use a recessed frame that allows space between the work and the glass and prevents the embroidery and attached flowers being flattened.

If you only have a standard frame, you can provide enough depth to keep the glass away from the work by layering two or three mounts on top of each other.

You can also remove the glass from an ordinary frame. If you do this, it is a good idea to spray the work, including the mount, with fabric protector to prevent it becoming dirty. This is available in sprays and is very easy to use. If you use fabric protector on your work, make sure you only use the spray outside or in a very-well ventilated room.

Poppies in the Corn

This picture has been mounted in a recessed frame, which you can buy ready-made or have made to size. The picture was completed, then mounted on a board. When you do this, make sure the board is bigger than the aperture of the frame, but no bigger than the outer edge. The mounted embroidery can then be stapled or stuck to the back of the frame to make sure it is well away from the glass.

Dyeing threads

The embroidery threads you can buy come in a wide range of colours as well as space-dyed or variegated options. The problem comes when you need to match threads you have bought with your own dyed work because the colours may be wrong. To make the threads more interesting and give a more realistic look that blends in with your individual piece of work, you can easily add a little dye to them. Subtle colour changes are the most effective. Use silk dyes, as these will take on any natural threads such as cotton, silk, linen or wool. Use the dye you have been using on your fabric, or make a fresh mix if necessary. You may need to water the dye it down a little or put more colour in to make a deeper shade.

1 Remove the labels from the threads and replace them with small elastic bands to stop them unwinding. Place the dyes in small, deep containers, using them neat or diluted: for this skein I am using purple and yellow.

2 Dip the end of the banded yarn in the first colour and hold it for a few seconds. Make sure it penetrates right to the centre of the skein.

3 Repeat the process with the other end of the skein of thread, dipping it into the second colour dye.

NOTE

If the colours look too pale when they have dried, you can simply add some more dye to the areas you want to enhance and leave the thread to dry again before continuing.

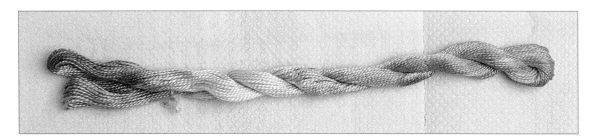

4 Place the skein on absorbent paper to dry. To set the dyes, use a hairdryer on maximum heat for five to ten minutes or place the skein in a warm oven for ten minutes and finally leave in a warm place for a day. A radiator is ideal, but make sure the skein is dry to the touch before you put it on or it may stain the radiator.

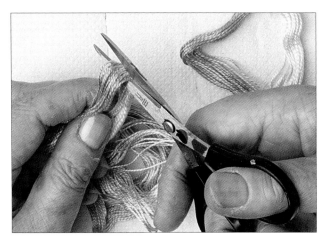

5 Unravel the skein and cut through one end of the loop, opposite the tied section.

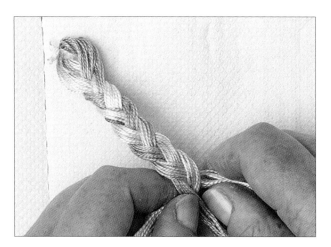

6 Plait the skein loosely and fasten off the end using a small elastic band.

A selection of threads, dyed and ready for use

Surface embroidery

None of the embroidery I use is difficult or precise, so do not worry if your eyesight is not perfect. I do not use fine threads, small stitches, fine needles, or stitch in straight lines. In nature, flowers move when the wind blows and there are no straight lines, so I try to capture this freedom in my embroidery.

There are many types of thread, but I mainly use two types, perlé and stranded, to obtain a variety of textures. You can divide stranded threads and use one, two, three or more of the strands. Perlé can be used double, or couched for a thicker effect. Work one stitch on top of another to add depth and more texture, or work the same stitch in another colour or a different thread. Experiment with those you have already.

Use an embroidery needle, with a large eye if you are using perlé thread or all six strands of stranded thread. I sometimes use chenille needles which have a sharp point and a large eye. When the thread is very thick I might even use a tapestry needle, though these can be difficult to pull through the work. Try not to pull the embroidery thread too tightly across the back of the work.

Work in the way you feel happiest: you may prefer to use an embroidery hoop when hand stitching. I do not, because I take my work with me when I am travelling, demonstrating, or even when I think that I might have to wait some time for a hospital or doctor's appointment! Backing it with fine wadding or an extra piece of cotton fabric will give your work some body.

Adding extra colour to threads gives them a more natural and interesting look, and if you use some of the colours from your painted backgrounds to do this it will help them to blend more effectively with your work – see page 26. When you have the colour on the background, you will find that it helps you to decide where to put your stitches. You do not have to cover every area with stitching, as the colours in your background fabric will also be part of the work.

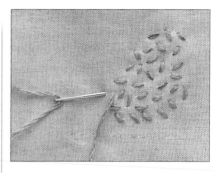

Seed stitch

For this stitch, bring the needle through to the front of the fabric, then take it through to the back again. The size of stitch will vary according to the type of thread and the effect you wish to produce. Vary the angle of the stitch for a random effect. It is ideal for adding texture and interest, and can be worked on top of machine embroidered areas.

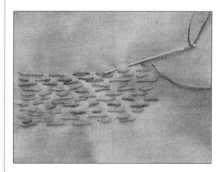

Running stitch

Insert the needle and bring it up again about 6mm (¼in) along. If you are embroidering grasses in simple running stitch, avoid straight lines and make the stitches uneven in length: if they are the same distance apart the grasses may not look realistic.

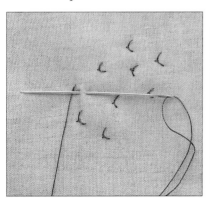

Fly stitch

This stitch can be worked in any size, so first decide how big you want your birds to be. I usually use dark grey sewing thread as black can look harsh. Bring the thread through to the front and insert it a short distance away. Bring it back up in the same place and take it over the thread before pushing it back through the work.

French knots

For the techniques in this book, this is the most important stitch to master. Used alone, it gives the impression of massed flowers, especially if worked with variegated thread and knots of different sizes. French knots make an attractive background for fabric 'flower' circles. This not only gives texture to your work, but also pushes the cut flowers up and out and makes them look realistic. To add extra depth and texture, I often put French knots on top of seed stitch or running stitch.

The diagram right shows a typical way to make French knots: bring the needle out at (A), hold the thread between thumb and forefinger and twist the needle round it twice (or more times as required). Then ease the needle back halfway at (B), pull the twist down the needle so that it lies against the fabric, and push the needle through to the back of the fabric.

Practise making French knots on a spare piece of fabric until you are comfortable with the technique. Step photograph 11 on page 33 shows me making one.

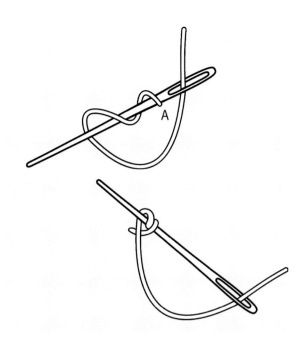

French knots (1)

These knots were worked using stranded thread which was dyed to produce a variegated effect.

French knots (2)

This example shows knots worked with two different colours of perlé thread.

Summer Meadow

This is a very simple project, which uses only dyes and hand stitched French knots. Even so, by the time you have completed this project, you will have the knowledge and skills to let your imagination run riot. No two backgrounds will ever look the same because of the way the dyes run, but this just adds to the unique quality of your embroideries.

Colour reference sketch
I did this sketch on holiday. It shows the colours and atmosphere of the golden glow in the sky that evening, contrasting with the reds and browns of the grasses.

You will need
- Pure cotton fabric 15 x 20 cm (6 x 8in)
- 2oz wadding in the same size to back your work
- Silk dye in yellow, red and black
- Black and red fabric pens
- Stranded embroidery thread: one skein each of yellow and black 13mm (½in) flat brush
- Masking tape
- Non-woven all-purpose household cloths
- Absorbent paper (optional)
- Scrap paper or newspaper
- Sewing needle and thread
- Iron
- Aperture mount 7 x 12cm (2¾ x 4¾in)
- Tacking cotton and needle

The dyes used for the project

Dyeing the background

You can place absorbent paper beneath your fabric before fixing it down with masking tape. This may give you an interesting paper background that can be used later (see page 62).

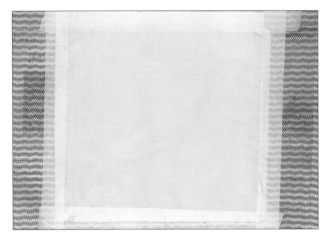

1 Protect your work surface with scrap paper and cover with all-purpose kitchen cloth. Press the fabric and secure it on top with masking tape. Using a 13mm (½in) flat wash brush, paint yellow dye evenly across the fabric.

2 Leave your work to dry. Paint the lower section of the cotton fabric with red dye, leaving room for this layer of dye to seep upwards. Leave to dry again.

3 Dilute the black dye with a little water and apply it to the lower third of the fabric as shown. Leave your work to dry, remembering that the colours will dry lighter.

TIP

If the colours look too pale when they have dried, simply add some more dye to the areas you want to enhance and leave to dry again before continuing.

4 Remove the masking tape. Cut out the section of background you want to use for your embroidery.

5 Using the black fabric pen draw some grasses which reach up to the middle section. Work over the black penned area with the red fabric pen. Leave to dry. With the iron set on cotton, press the fabric to set the dyes.

6 Lay the piece of wadding behind your work and tack/baste all around the edge to hold it in place.

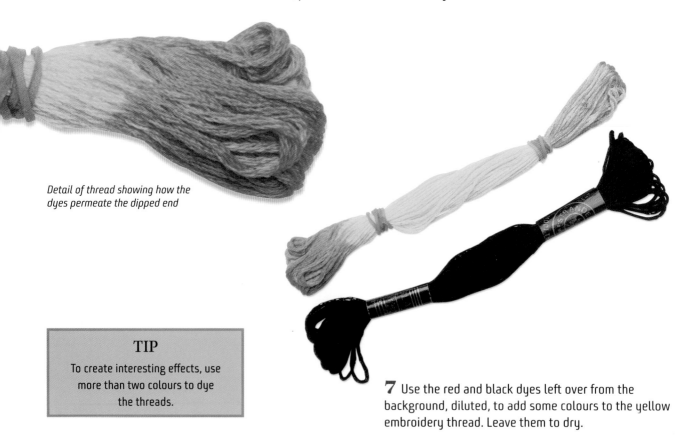

Detail of thread showing how the dyes permeate the dipped end

TIP
To create interesting effects, use more than two colours to dye the threads.

7 Use the red and black dyes left over from the background, diluted, to add some colours to the yellow embroidery thread. Leave them to dry.

8 Trim off the excess wadding using sharp scissors.

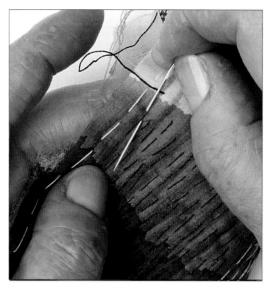

9 Using one strand of black stranded embroidery thread, make short uneven running stitches on top of the drawn grasses.

10 Using one strand of yellow thread, add some more running stitches to the top area of the grasses.

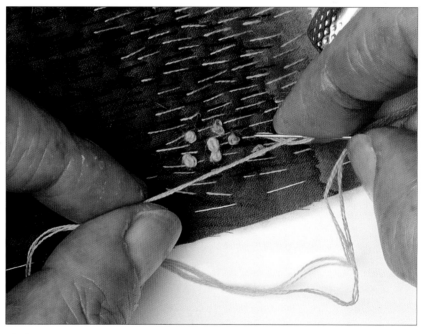

11 Place French knots randomly in clusters over the middle and upper area of the grasses. Vary the number of strands of thread used, and make thicker knots near the bottom to give the appearance of depth. When I make a French knot, I hold the thread taut as I wind the thread round the needle. Then I insert the point of the needle and pull the thread gently until the wound threads are sitting on the surface of the work in the correct position. Still holding the thread, I push the needle through to the back of the work. This method helps to prevent the threads tangling as the stitch is worked.

Detail of embroidered birds – see page 34

The finished picture

The Mottled Sky

Size: 18 x 23cm (7 x 9in)

I sprinkled salt on the background sky while it was still very wet. I drew in grasses using fabric pen before adding French knots for the flowers. To do this, I used thread that had been dyed with several colours, placing them very closely together for a massed effect. I used thick, variegated thread for the stems of the flowers.

Detail of background

The background for this picture was begun in exactly the same way as for the preceding project, but I used salt on the sky area while it was still wet, to discharge the colour and give the sky a mottled effect.

Machine embroidery

Free motion machine embroidery could be described as drawing with a needle, except that the work rather than the needle moves. You will soon become used to the different way of working. This method is easy for beginners to follow, but if you have never done any free motion embroidery before, practise on a small piece first. I have used only basic straight and zig-zag stitch, which most machines are able to do.

When you use a machine in the normal way, the teeth or dog feed move backwards and forwards, pulling the fabric through. For free machine embroidery, you disable this function by dropping the teeth to darning position and move the fabric yourself. Sometimes a plate is provided to cover the dog feed. If not, just make your own by cutting some firm card and taping it in position over the teeth.

The function of a standard machine foot is to hold the work in place while the teeth move it under the needle. You will need to change this for an embroidery or darning foot which will let you move your work freely. There may be one or more supplied with your machine, or you can buy one separately. If you do not have a suitable foot you can work without one, but you must make sure that you have the foot lever in the down position. Note that if you do this your fingers will have no protection, so keep them well clear of the moving needle.

Thread your sewing machine in the usual way. Loosen the top tension a little to make sure the bobbin thread does not show through, then you will not need to change the colour on the bobbin thread.
Keep your work taut by tacking it on to paper or heavy, non-woven interfacing, or place it in an embroidery frame small enough to move round easily on the machine.

Metal ring frame

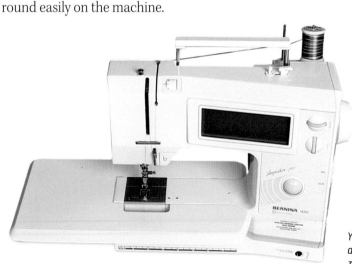

You will need only a very basic machine and it need not produce fancy stitches. Zig-zag stitch is useful, but not essential.

Stitches

It will be far easier to work out where to put your machine stitches when you have put the fabric dyes and paints on your fabric. Remember that you do not have to cover all the fabric with stitch, just the areas that you want to make more interesting.

Set the machine for free machine embroidery (see page 36). Place your work in an embroidery hoop or tack it to a few sheets of photocopier paper to stiffen it. Use a medium to heavy needle (size 14–16) and keep your work moving while you are sewing, or the threads may tangle on the back and jam your machine. If you work on paper, remember that the needle may go blunt more quickly. All examples are worked with green variegated thread.

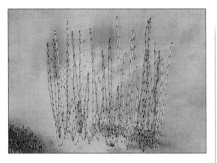

Grasses

To give the effect of grasses, use straight stitch and turn your work sideways. As you machine, move the work from right to left and vice versa.

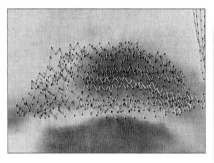

Foliage

To work shrubs and trees, set the machine to a medium-width zig-zag. Move your work backwards and forwards as you machine. This is also a good background for hand stitching.

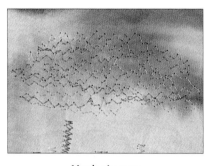

Mock zig-zag

If your machine will not do zig-zag, you can produce a similar effect with straight stitch. As you stitch, move the work from left to right as well as backwards and forwards. It is hard to spot the difference!

Grass stems

Set the sewing machine to medium zig-zag stitch. Move the work towards you, then away from you, then back again to complete each stem. The example is worked in variegated green thread, so that the grass stems looks like they are growing in different shades.

Grass stems (2)

Though it looks very similar to the last example, this was worked on a sewing machine with no zig-zag stitch. Use straight stitch and move the work to the left and right as well as backwards and forwards. You will soon master the technique.

Backgrounds

The backgrounds on this page were created by brushing two shades of silk dye on to the fabric, blue and mauve, using different dilutions of the colours. They were then embroidered by machine.

You do not have to use machine stitching, which in any case will mostly be covered with hand stitch later. The benefit of machine embroidery is that the small amounts that do show through add depth and interest to your finished picture.

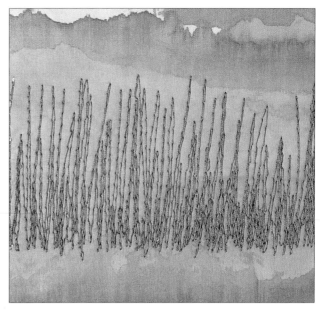

With the sewing machine set up for free machine embroidery and set on straight stitch, I moved the work back and forward to produce the grass.

This time I added flowers to the top of the grasses using medium zig-zag stitch and mauve variegated machine thread, again moving the work backwards and forwards under the machine.

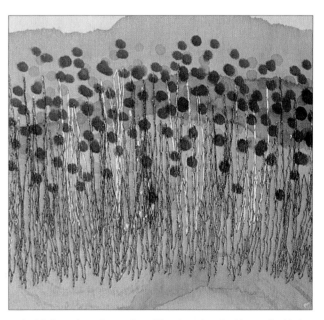

I added purple variegated machine thread to the blue and added purple and blue dots with the top of a fabric pen.

Blue Flowers

Size: 16 x 21 (6¼ x 8¼in)

The background for this embroidery was produced using the techniques on the previous page. It is a good example of the different effects that can be achieved by varying the tones and colours of the backgrounds and embroidery.

Buttercup Field

This project introduces free motion machine embroidery. Machine embroidery can be left as it is or you can hand-embroider over the top. If you choose to do this, small areas of machine embroidery will peep through the hand embroidery and it is surprising how much extra depth this will give to your picture.

The project uses only two dye colours, blue and yellow, but you will see how many colour variations and shades this can produce. Allowing the dyes to blend, mixing and thinning them and laying one transparent layer on top of another will produce a wide variety of colour.

If you do not have a sewing machine, or do not wish to carry out machine embroidery, this project can be completed with hand embroidery only.

This bank of yellow flowers was the inspiration for the project

You will need

- White cotton fabric 30 x 25cm (12 x 10in)
- White cotton fabric for the flowers 15 x 15cm (6 x 6in)
- 2oz wadding 30 x 25cm (12 x 10in)
- Blue and yellow silk dyes
- Containers for mixing dye
- Black fabric pen
- Yellow stranded embroidery thread
- Green variegated machine embroidery thread
- Dark grey sewing thread
- Sewing and embroidery needles
- Brush No 5
- All-purpose cloth
- Masking tape
- Sewing machine
- Embroidery hoop
- Scrap paper or newspaper
- Absorbent paper (optional)
- Iron for pressing

The dyes used for the background

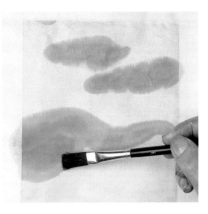

NOTE

You can place absorbent paper under the fabric before fixing it down with masking tape. This may give you some interesting paper to work on later (see page 62).

1 Lay scrap paper or newspaper on your work surface with all-purpose kitchen cloth on top, and fix your fabric on to this with masking tape. Add water to the blue dye until it is very pale, and use a flat wash brush to cover the fabric. Leave to dry.

2 Add a little more blue dye to the mix to deepen the colour. Paint most of the lower half, plus some areas at the top. Leave to dry. Drying time will vary according to humidity and the temperature of the room.

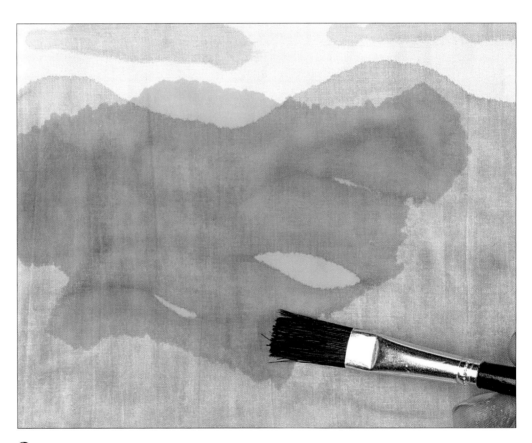

3 Thin the yellow dye with a little cold water to give a paler shade, and paint it on the lower half of the fabric. The blue will show through, so it will look green. Leave to dry.

4 Mix a slightly darker shade of blue dye and overpaint parts of the lower area, so that they go a darker shade of green. Leave your work until it is dry to the touch. The time it takes to do this will vary depending on the room temperature and the thickness of the fabric used.

NOTE

The measurements allow surplus fabric, so you will have ample to put on your hoop when machining. This means that there is no need to take the dyes right to the edge of the fabric.

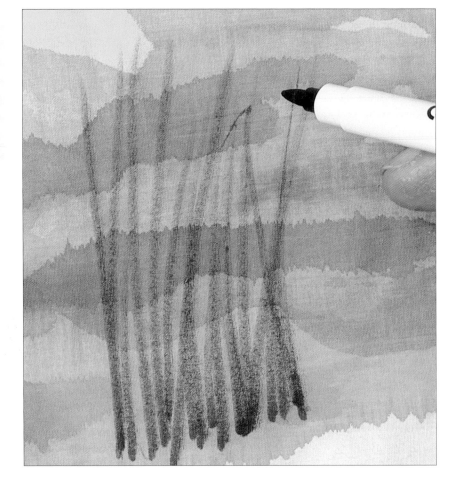

5 Use black fabric pen to draw in some grasses. Make them look natural by keeping them uneven and putting in a few extra lines at the bottom to give a thicker effect. Allow to dry, then press your work to set the dyes.

6 Add a small amount of blue dye to the yellow embroidery thread which will be used to embroider the flowers. This will add some subtle darker tones to the thread. Set aside to dry.

7 With yellow dye mix used for the background, cover the small piece of cotton fabric reserved for the cut flower circles.

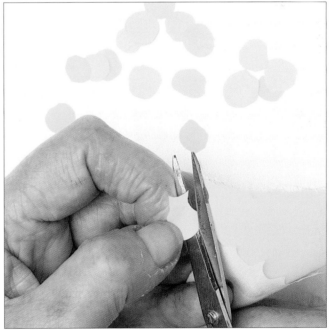

8 While the painted fabric is still damp, add random drops of blue dye to give the cut flowers more interest. Allow to dry, then iron to set the dyes.

9 Cut circles approximately 1cm (³⁄₈in) diameter from the yellow fabric. Do not try to make them all exactly the same size: they will look more natural if they vary slightly.

NOTE

If you want to use a sewing machine, set it up for free machine embroidery (see page 36) using green variegated machine embroidery thread. Practise on a spare piece of material first: the stitches should look quite free and some areas should be stitched more densely. Vary the angle of some of the machine stitches slightly. Remember that you can also complete this stage by hand using one or two strands of green hand embroidery thread – see page 33 for a hand stitch that will produce a similar effect.

10 Back the work with the wadding or backing fabric, and tack it in place. With the green variegated thread, embroider grasses on the lower section as shown. If you use a machine, place your work in an embroidery hoop, and make sure it is taut. Turn your work sideways and move the frame from left to right and vice versa. Repeat until you have completed the areas you want to embroider. Press your work.

11 Using three strands of the dip-dyed yellow stranded embroidery thread, place French knots randomly over most of the lower area. These can be in different sizes and thicknesses. This can be achieved by the number of times you wind the thread around the needle, or the number of strands of thread used.

NOTE
Try not to pull the threads too tight when stitching on flowers by hand. Place your work in an embroidery frame if this helps you work more comfortably.

12 Work over the area you have covered in French knots and attach the cut-out circles using a double back stitch in the centre of each one. You can also sew on the flowers using a few machine stitches in the centre of each. The French knots on the background will push the flowers out to give a realistic 3D effect.

13 With the dark grey sewing thread, add a few small detached fly stitches to represent birds in flight (see page 28 for method).

The bigger picture

Once you become used to completing embroideries, you might like to produce a panoramic picture, or work on a larger piece which you can cut into more than one picture for framing. To do this, I work the embroidery in exactly the same way, but I use a wider piece of background fabric. This method is ideal for producing panoramic scenes like the ones on pages 3, 48–9, 73 and 76–78.

Work in progress

This example shows work in progress on a long strip of material which could be cut into smaller sections to make more than one picture. These can then be mounted using the method on page 24.

Opposite

The finished picture

Do not press your work, as you may flatten the flowers.
To mount your work, follow the steps on page 24.

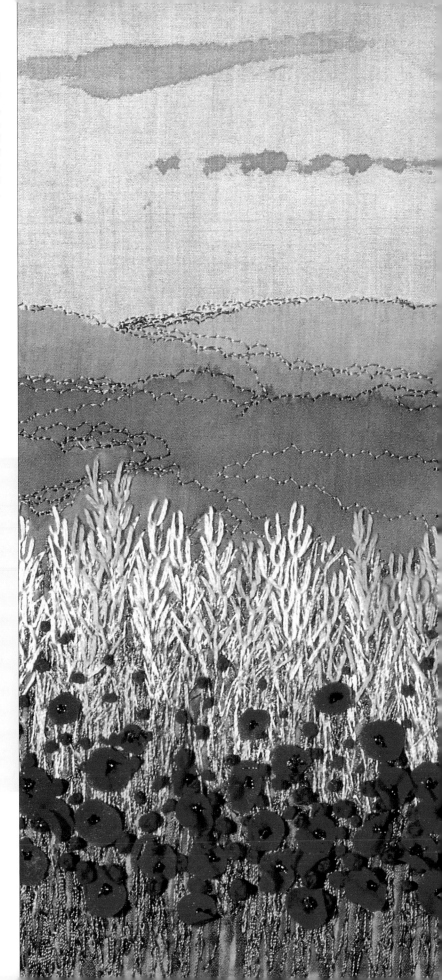

Poppy Field

Size: 26 x 22cm (10 x 8½in)

The background for this picture was painted in exactly the same way as for the Buttercup project, but the when the grasses were drawn I added green and red lines as well. Machine and hand stitching was added over the top. The applied flowers were sewn on by machine, using a dark grey lurex machine embroidery thread to give a sparkly effect.

Detail of background

The background used to produce the embroidery. The grasses have been drawn in using fabric pens in black, green and red.

48

Flowers by the Fence

This project will add three new skills to those learned in previous sections: salting, spongeing and masking. It uses a simple resist method with masking tape. This means that the fabric is resistant to the next colour applied and, when the tape is removed, will reveal the last colour you used. This basic method can be used to produce some very impressive results.

    The instructions that follow are just guidelines. You may have some similar colour fabric dye and fabric paint and the thread colours maybe different. Do not worry, it will work just the same. No two skies will be the same, as the salt discharge is unpredictable, as is the sponging. In fact your picture will be individual and a one-off.

The sketch I used for inspiration

You will need

For the background:
- White cotton fabric 30 x 25cm (12 x 10in)
- White cotton fabric for the flowers 15 x 15cm (6 x 6in)
- Fine cotton backing fabric 40 x 35cm (16 x 14in)
- 2oz wadding 30 x 25cm (12 x 10in)
- Silk dyes: mauve, brown and magenta
- Fabric paint: dark green, yellow and magenta
- Several small sponges
- Masking tape 2cm (¾in) wide
- Flat wash brush size 5
- All-purpose cloth
- Newspaper
- Bubble wrap
- Dishwasher salt
- Scissors
- Iron

For the machine embroidery
- Machine sewing thread: lime green and variegated green
- Embroidery hoop

For the hand embroidery
- Stranded embroidery thread: light green, green perlé and magenta

For mounting
- Aperture mount 17 x 23cm (6¾ x 9in)
- A few sheets of photocopier paper

The dyes and paints I used for the project

1 Protect your work surface with scrap paper or newspaper. Lay all-purpose kitchen cloth on top and secure the fabric on this with masking tape. Apply a pale wash of mauve silk dye to the top half of the fabric and sprinkle small areas immediately with dishwasher salt. Leave for at least 20 minutes.

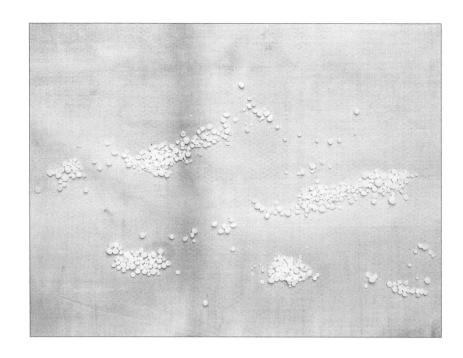

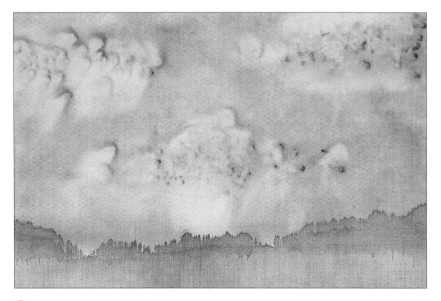

NOTE

You should not use absorbent paper under this project, as the fabric paints may stick to the paper when it dries.

2 Brush the salt from the fabric. It will look mottled with lighter areas where the salt has absorbed some of the dye. Apply a wash of pale, watered-down brown silk dye to the bottom half of the fabric. Leave to dry.

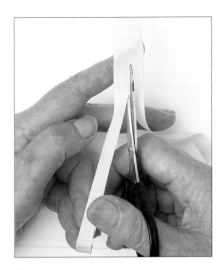 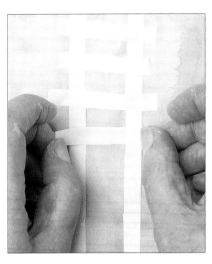

3 Using scissors, cut a piece of masking tape the same width as the background fabric. Cut through the tape lengthways.

4 Place the two strips 3cm (1¼in) apart across your work. Cut smaller pieces of masking tape to make the fence posts and space evenly across your work.

5 Make sure the masking tape is pressed firmly into place.

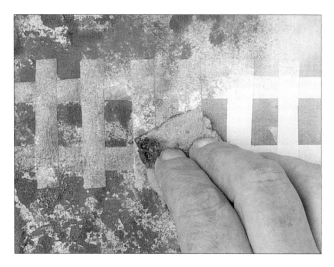

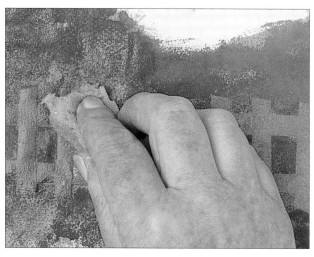

6 Using a small piece of sponge, dab on dark green fabric paint gently so you do not pull off the masking tape. Remove surplus paint from the sponge before using it on your work.

7 With a clean sponge dab on the yellow paint. Cover all the areas that are not covered with the green paint.

8 When dry, remove the masking tape to reveal the brown fence.

9 Cut a piece of bubble wrap into an uneven shape and use a paint brush to cover it with magenta fabric paint.

10 Turn the painted bubble wrap over and use it to print circular impressions on to the lower part of the fence. Put aside to dry.

11 Cut another piece of bubble wrap and cover it with green fabric paint, then repeat the printing process. When you have achieved the effect you want, leave your work to dry.

12 While the background fabric is drying, take the spare piece of cotton fabric and cover it with magenta silk dye (not fabric paint). Leave it to dry, then iron it to set the dye. Cut it into circles approximately 1cm (³⁄₈in) in diameter for the flowers.

13 Place 2oz wadding behind your work, then place on the backing fabric which is about 6cm (2½in) larger all round to provide a border for ease of working. Tack round the edge, then machine stitch in place. Prepare the sewing machine for free machine embroidery, using green variegated thread. Place your work in an embroidery hoop. Stitch over the green area above the fence, to give the impression of a hill and trees. Move the hoop to different areas of your work as necessary.

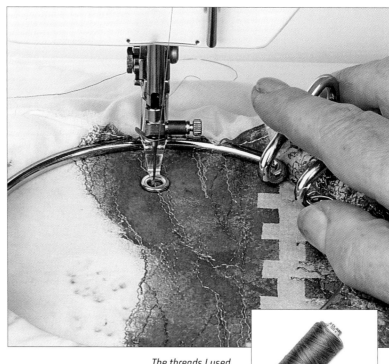

The threads I used

NOTE

If your machine does not have a zig-zag facility, use straight stitch, but move the fabric under the needle to produce an irregular effect.

14 Move the embroidery hoop to the lower area and set the machine for medium width zig-zag stitch. Machine over the whole area to give the impression of grasses and foliage round the flowers. Some of the printed colours will show through the machining. The light green machine thread can be used to pick out some of the lighter areas.

The threads used for the French knots have been dipped in the mauve and the magenta dyes and allowed to dry.

15 Embroider French knots on the lower half of your work, varying their size and thickness by using more strands or winding the yarn round the needle more times. Use magenta and green stranded embroidery threads.

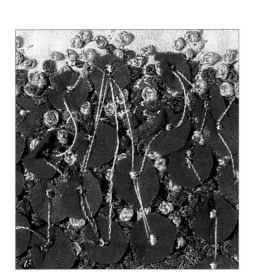

16 Apply the cut flowers by machine using a small zig-zag stitch in the centre of each flower. You can also sew them on by hand using a double back stitch.

17 Trim the threads between the flowers when you have finished. Do not press your work afterwards, or you will flatten the flowers.

The finished picture

The picture has been completed by the addition of birds worked using dark grey thread and fly stitch (see page 28). More French knots or applied flowers can be added at any stage before mounting.

If you want to frame your work, place a mount over the area you want to use for the finished picture. Trim, leaving enough fabric all around to attach to the back of the mount (see page 24).

Garden Gate

Size: 18 x 23cm (7 x 9in)

I added a 'gate' to this picture when placing the masking tape. I did not use salt on the sky in this picture. I painted the sky and let it dry, then to add interest, I deepened the intensity of the mix of dye and lightly dragged the brush across. The stems of the flowers were embroidered using a perlé thread and the work was completed with flowers cut from fabric dyed with a mix of blue and magenta dye.

The Fence

Size: 18 x 23cm (7 x 9in)

For this fast and simple variation on the garden fence picture, I used the self-adhesive grid left over from a finished book of postage stamps. Only hand stitching has been used for this piece.

NOTE

When you have used adhesive labels or stickers, the waste can be just as useful. This is the grid left after postage stamps have been removed.

Near the End of the Day

Size: 30 x 25cm (12 x 10in)

I dyed the background in the usual way using yellow, green and black dyes. It was then machine embroidered before overprinting with magenta and mauve fabric paint and small-size bubble wrap. The work is still being finished with French knots, using coordinating coloured thread. Comparison of the printed and unprinted sections shows how the hand stitching brings the work to life.

Embroidered cards

I make a lot of cards using small scraps of work left over from larger projects, or pieces salvaged from projects that have not turned out quite as I expected. In this way, I can make beautiful cards more quickly, and as I never like to waste anything I really enjoy doing it.

I also make cards from something most people would throw away: the pieces of absorbent paper that I use under my fabric backgrounds. This paper is put there to absorb some of the dye, but I discovered that it takes on patterns similar to those painted on the fabric above. Many of these are interesting in their own right, and as it seemed a shame to throw them away I began to experiment with them.

You will need

· Absorbent paper used beneath other projects
· Machine embroidery threads
· Spray adhesive
· Plain white paper
· Scrap paper or newspaper

Embroidering on paper

The method I have worked out is easy: when you have finished a fabric background and it is completely dry, separate the absorbent paper carefully from the fabric instead of throwing it away. If you mount it on plain paper using spray adhesive, you will be able to embroider on it. Machine embroidery produces fast results. It is not really advisable to hand stitch on as the paper may tear. The machine-embroidered pieces can then simply be cut up and mounted in ready-made card mounts.

The absorbent paper used beneath the Buttercup field project on page 40.

1 Protect the work surface with scrap paper and cover the back of the absorbent paper with spray adhesive.

2 Place the absorbent paper on a sheet of plain white paper to stiffen it. Prepare the machine for free machine embroidery and embroider straight on to the paper.

NOTE
Make sure you use spray adhesive outside or in a well ventilated room.

The finished cards
After embroidering, the absorbent paper was cut to size and placed in ready-made card mounts.

Paper landscape

After selecting a suitable area to work on, I fixed it to firmer paper using spray adhesive. I used my sewing machine and variegated green machine embroidery thread to make the grass stems. I added zig-zag stitch to represent the flowers. The finished piece can be mounted (see page 24) and displayed, or fixed to a greetings card blank. You could even add a calendar and give it as a seasonal gift.

Opposite

Greetings cards

A selection of cards made with fabric and paper backgrounds.

Taking things further

The different techniques in this book can be used in any combination, whether you use only hand stitch, a mixture of hand or machine stitch, or even no stitch at all. When you use a simple resist like a label or a piece of masking tape, remember that it will allow the colour underneath it to show through after you have removed the resist, so the colour can be used as part of the design. The colour you use first is as important as the layer of paints or dyes that go on top. I usually use silk dyes for the background, as you can blend and layer them and the fabric will stay soft and pliable. Too many layers of fabric paint can make the fabric stiff and therefore harder to stitch on.

Poppies

An extra touch can be added by painting in the hole in the centre of the ring reinforcement. Red and yellow fabric paint was dabbed on the lower areas and allowed to dry. The ring reinforcements were placed on the red area and sponged over with green fabric paint. Black paint was added to the centre of the rings.

RING REINFORCEMETS

These can be used as a resist.

Background

White cotton was dabbed with pale blue fabric paint so that some of the material showed through, then the lower section was dabbed with a deeper blue fabric paint to form the background for the hollyhocks.

This background was dyed yellow and self-adhesive dots placed on top. Green and blue fabric paint was sponged over and left to dry before the dots were removed.

SELF-ADHESIVE DOTS

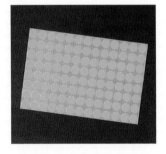

These can also be used as a simple form of resist to mask areas of your work.

Hollyhocks

When it was dry, I added self-adhesive dots and dabbed over fabric paint in shades of green. The dots were removed to reveal the blue underneath, and I added French knots in blue to complete the impression of flowers.

This comes in a range of bubble sizes.

In Blossom

Size: 13 x 18cm (5 x 7in)

The background was dyed with blue silk dye, with small touches of pale purple added to create the sky and brown dye placed on the lower part. When the background was dry the label grids were placed on. Bubble wrap with 'baby' bubbles was used to overprint the blossom in pale blue and pink. The work was finished using a pink machine embroidery thread and random machine stitches.

Opposite

Country Garden

Size: 13 x 18cm (5 x 7in)

This array of flowers was achieved with fabric pen lines over a background of silk dyed cotton fabric. This was overprinted using bubble wrap and pearlised fabric paint. It was then machine embroidered with green and magenta thread and green perlé thread, to which I had added some magenta dye. The flowers were brought to life by adding French knots using variegated stranded thread.

DYED LACE

Lace that has been dyed and cut into circles produces interesting flower effects.

Lavender and Lace

Size: 13 x 18cm (5 x 7in)

The background fabric of this picture was dyed with silk dyes, then fabric pens were used for the grass. It was machine stitched and overprinted using blue and mauve fabric paint on bubble wrap. Pieces of dyed lace were applied instead of circles of fabric to produce a more delicate flower effect. This is an interesting way to give flowers a different texture, and inexpensive bundles of lace are readily available from market stalls. Some fabric dyes are suitable for use on man-made fibres, so you can use them to dye fine nylon lace. Check the manufacturer's recommendations.

Growing Along the River

Size: 17 x 17cm (6¾ x 6¾in)

The background of this picture was created by using masking tape to create a clear line between the river and the hills. Star-shaped stickers were placed on the foreground, which was then dabbed with a green fabric paint. The effect was completed with French knots and applied flowers cut from lace that was dyed green.

STAR STICKERS

These are ideal for producing interesting flower effects.

Moody Loch

Size: 25.5 x 33cm (10 x 13in)

This was inspired by the glow of the sky after a chilly day walking by the loch. Just before night fell, the moody sky cast a glow over the water. I added machine stitch over the dark hills to pick out some of the areas of interest. The water was machine embroidered with gold lurex machine thread before adding the hand stitch and applied flowers.

I also used some batik to detail the flowers and the water. I often use batik, which is a hot wax resist applied with a brush or a tool with a spout called a canting. The use of batik requires specialist knowledge and a lot of practice, plus special equipment. It works much like the masking tape method, in that the wax preserves the colour that is covered.

Opposite

Purples and Pinks

Size: 13 x 18cm (5 x 7in)

The pale pink foreground flowers stand out against the deep purple of the sky. I dyed the background using a darker shade at the top. It was machine embroidered with blending machine thread in greens and pinks. The applied flowers were cut from a piece of an old clean cotton lace curtain, which was dyed with a mixture of pink and pale purple silk dye. I dyed the embroidery threads I used for the French knots at the same time as the background.

Paper mounts

One of the most interesting ways to use machine embroidery is for the technique shown on these pages. Complete the background of your piece of work using fabric dyes, paints, hand and machine embroidery, then cut it carefully to size and place it on hand-made paper. The work can be pinned into place, or fixed with spray adhesive. The best paper to use is paper made from cotton or linen, or containing long fibres, as it will be less likely to tear when sewn on.

Stitch around the four sides using a close satin stitch. Any colour thread can be used, but for the work shown I have used metallic thread. When you have machined the picture in place, use a fabric pen to extend the drawn grasses out of the picture and on to the paper. Complete your picture by extending the embroidery from the fabric over the paper, and adding cut circles by hand or machine.

Opposite

Pink Hue

Size: 18 x 26cm (7 x 10in)

This was completed using the same techniques as the picture opposite, but the birds were embroidered on to the fabric before it was stitched to the hand-made paper. The birds on the paper were drawn with black pen.

Towards the Copse

Size: 18 x 22.5cm (7 x 9in)

The background was dyed using turquoise and mauve silk dyes for the sky, and green shades for the foliage. I dyed a spare piece of fabric with magenta silk dye for the fabric circles. Both machine and hand embroidery were added before I applied the fabric circles.

The picture was then machine stitched on to hand-made paper. The picture was extended onto the paper with fabric pens and machine embroidery, and the cut flowers added by machine using a small zig-zag stitch in the centre of each.

The final touch was the addition of a few birds in gold fabric pen, which were taken out of the picture on to the paper mount.

Panoramic scenes

The backgrounds for these panoramic scenes were produced using the techniques you have already learned. It is a good idea to cut the fabric to a slightly larger size than you plan for the finished picture, so that there is some leeway when it comes to choosing the best area to use. The water for these pictures was machine embroidered using gold lurex thread, then the grasses were added by machining vertically over the edge of the water. French knots were added to give the impression of massed flowers.

Mauve in the Sky
Size: 48 x 18cm (19 x 7in)

This picture was inspired by the long panoramic view looking out across the sea, after a peaceful day walking along the coast. I added a touch of mauve dye to the sky, to help it blend with the mauve and blues of the flowers The work was stitched on to hand-made paper, then extended at the sides and bottom by the addition of more flowers and grasses.

Flowers of Fire
Size: 48 x 18cm (19 x 7in)

When the setting sun vanishes below the horizon it can leave a mixture of dramatic colours in the sky. I have tried to capture this using red, yellow, and blue, set against the simple bright red of the flowers in the foreground. The completed picture was machine-sewn on to hand-made paper, and the flowers were extended over the paper a little at the sides to produce a dramatic effect.

Conclusion

I have shown you simple and versatile techniques – now it is up to you to use them as creatively as you can. The projects will help you to learn and practise, but they are really just a starting point so you can let your creative imagination run riot. Change the colours, and you can make your own stunning personal piece of work. Why not try incorporating other skills such as feltmaking, crochet, tatting, beading and lacemaking? Small areas of beadwork or crochet can add interest, and if you are interested in stumpwork, you might like to embroider raised flowers or leaves among the cut flowers. A lace maker might want to make flowers with fine random dyed thread instead of cutting them out, or you could try framing your work with a hand-dyed patchwork.

To mask out areas for the work shown in this book, I have used simple resist methods including tape and labels. I often use batik for my own work, but this technique would probably need a book of its own. The concept of resist used in this book is basically similar, though it has some limitations.

The work featured is made predominantly with the methods shown in the three projects. The possibilities are endless.

Remember that no piece is ever a failure, as you will always find an area, no matter how small, that you can salvage. This can be made into a picture – even if it is smaller than you intended – or a greetings card for someone special.

Sunset Over the Banks

Size: 28 x 21cm (11 x 8¼in)

This piece of work used only the methods shown in this book, so as you can see you can accomplish very beautiful pictures by using the skill you have learnt and a little imagination.

Index